SPECIAL REPORTS

THE WAR ON POVERTY

BY CAROLEE LAINE

CONTENT CONSULTANT
MICHAEL J. RICH
PROFESSOR OF POLITICAL SCIENCE AND
ENVIRONMENTAL SCIENCES
EMORY UNIVERSITY

Essential Library
An Imprint of Abdo Publishing | abdopublishing.com

abdopublishing.com

Published by Abdo Publishing, a division of ABDO, PO Box 398166, Minneapolis, Minnesota 55439.

Printed in the United States of America, North Mankato, Minnesota
082016
012017

Cover Photo: Jake May/Flint Journal/AP Images
Interior Photos: Paul Beaty/AP Images, 4–5; John Minchillo/AP Images, 7; Mike Groll/AP Images, 9; Sharon Gekosi-Kimmel/KRT/Newscom, 13; Red Line Editorial, 15, 49, 72, 81; Jim West/Alamy, 18–19, 55, 94; M. Spencer Green/AP Images, 21; Matt York/AP Images, 26; Joyce Marshall/The Fort-Worth Telegram/AP Images, 31; AP Images, 32–33, 38; Thomas J. O'Halloran/Library of Congress, 35; Everett Collection/Newscom, 41; Lane V. Erickson/Shutterstock Images, 44–45; Adolphe Pierre-Louis/ZumaPress/Newscom, 47; Charles Dharapak/AP Images, 56–57; Chuck Kennedy/KRT/Newscom, 59; Jon-Michael Sullivan/The Augusta Chronicle/AP Images, 61; Cathy Bussewitz/AP Images, 64; Melanie Stetson Freeman/The Christian Science Monitor/AP Images, 68–69; Henry Burroughs/AP Images, 70; Jim West imageBROKER/Newscom, 75; imageBROKER/Alamy Stock Photo, 78–79; Ton Koene/Picture-Alliance/DPA/AP Images, 83; Bryan R. Smith/AP Images, 89; Jonathan Miano/The Times/AP Images, 90–91; Richard Vogel/AP Images, 93

Editor: Mirella Miller
Series Designer: Maggie Villaume

Publisher's Cataloging-in-Publication Data

Names: Laine, Carolee, author.
Title: The war on poverty / by Carolee Laine.
Description: Minneapolis, MN : Abdo Publishing, 2017. | Series: Special reports | Includes bibliographical references and index.
Identifiers: LCCN 2016945409 | ISBN 9781680783995 (lib. bdg.) | ISBN 9781680797527 (ebook)
Subjects: LCSH: Poverty--Government policy--United States--Juvenile literature | Economic assistance, Domestic--United States--Juvenile literature. | United States--Economic policy--Juvenile literature.
Classification: DDC 362.5--dc23
LC record available at http://lccn.loc.gov/2016945409

CONTENTS

WHO ARE THE POOR?

Alvin Major worked three jobs at fast-food restaurants in Brooklyn, New York. At a salary of $7.25 an hour, even his 80-hour workweeks could barely support his four children and his wife, who had been diagnosed with cancer.

In November 2012, Major took action. He joined 200 New York City fast-food workers in a mass walkout. "We decided we couldn't remain silent any longer," Major said. "We were going to go on strike."[1] The workers demanded $15 an hour, and the "Fight for $15" soon became a nationwide movement to raise pay for millions of low-wage workers.

Those workers included Dominique McCrae, who worked at a fast-food restaurant in Durham, North

Fast-food workers in Chicago, Illinois, protest for a higher minimum wage.

FIGHT FOR 15
FIGHT FOR 15

Carolina, for $7.55 an hour. The 23-year-old dropped out of college to care for her child and her grandfather. "We just want to be able to support our families," she said.[2] Another worker was Kheila Cox, a 38-year-old mother of seven who earned $10 an hour as a baggage handler in Boston, Massachusetts. "It's not just the financial piece," Cox said, "it's also about the dignity."[3]

THE FACES OF POVERTY

Common images of the poor include homeless men and women, transporting everything they own in a bag or a cart, sleeping on park benches or in makeshift shelters in the poorest parts of a city. They include people lined up at soup kitchens for a meal or begging on a street corner with a sign that reads, "Will work for food." Television documentaries take viewers into impoverished rural areas where families, defeated by poverty, live in shacks without running water or electricity. These are the poor, but they are not the only faces of poverty.

The phrase *the poor* implies that people who live in poverty are a single group, but that is inaccurate. Some groups of people and some locations have higher rates of

People living in poverty can include veterans, children, and disabled people.

poverty than others, but poverty is not limited to one race, age group, or gender. It is not confined to one location; it is global. Sometimes poverty is obvious, and sometimes it is invisible.

Harley Shaiken, a labor expert at the University of California, Berkeley, commented on the low-wage protesters in Los Angeles, California, "For many of us, these are workers who we see every day, yet they're invisible. What the Fight for 15 has done is give faces, names and personal stories that many, perhaps most, working Americans can identify with."[4]

FROM THE HEADLINES

THE FIGHT FOR $15

The campaign to raise the minimum wage to $15 an hour began in 2012. The Service Employees International Union (SEIU) supported it. Workers from fast-food chains, such as McDonald's and Taco Bell, took part in several protests for higher wages and the right to join a union.

On November 10, 2015, the protest became a daylong strike that involved thousands of workers in cities across the country. It included restaurant workers as well as low-paid hourly employees in other industries such as home care, childcare, nursing homes, hotels, and delivery services.

Unlike previous rallies, the November 10 protest had a political and economic purpose. Demonstrators gathered outside the Senate in Washington, DC, and outside local city halls to influence politicians at the federal and local levels. They protested at the Republican presidential debate in Milwaukee, Wisconsin. Workers pledged not to vote for presidential candidates who did not support the Fight for $15. They indicated they would hold voter registration drives to increase the number of workers who would use their influence in the 2016 election.

Opponents of the $15 minimum wage pointed out that many cities and states already had a minimum wage higher than the federal level of $7.25. They also argued that low-wage jobs in industries such as fast-food chains are not intended to be a lifelong career. Business owners indicated they could not afford to double the minimum wage to meet the demands of the workers. As a result, jobs would be cut.

Supporters of raising the minimum wage marched on November 10, 2015.

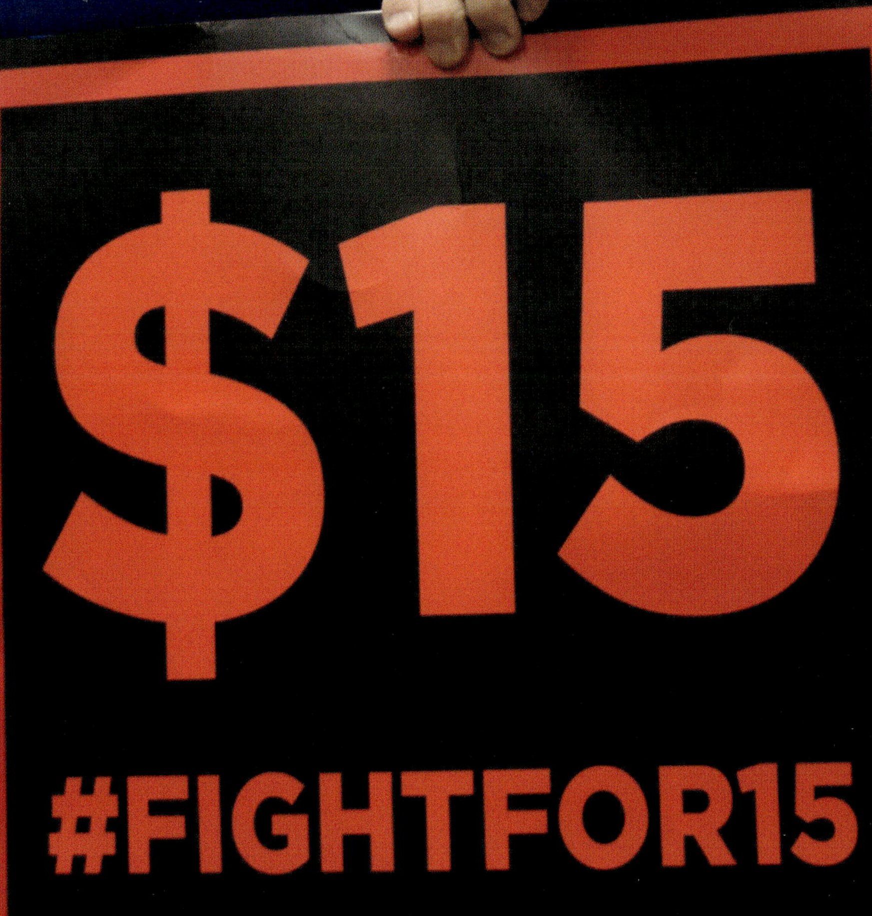

THE INVISIBLE POOR

In 1962, Michael Harrington wrote *The Other America*—a book that shed light on what it was like to be poor in the United States. The book became a classic work with a lasting influence. In it, Harrington describes what he calls the "invisible poor." These were the people who lived in rural areas where tourists did not visit or in miserable slums in isolated parts of cities. He argues that clothes made the poor invisible since inexpensive clothing was easier to afford than food, housing, or medical care. Even though people looked well-dressed, they were poor because they did not have enough money for other necessities.

"THAT THE POOR ARE INVISIBLE IS ONE OF THE MOST IMPORTANT THINGS ABOUT THEM. THEY ARE NOT SIMPLY NEGLECTED AND FORGOTTEN AS IN THE OLD RHETORIC OF REFORM; WHAT IS MUCH WORSE, THEY ARE NOT SEEN."[5]

—MICHAEL HARRINGTON, *THE OTHER AMERICA*, 1962

Fifty years after Harrington's book was published, many of the poor were still invisible, but for different reasons. A 2001 US Census Bureau survey reported that many Americans with incomes below the poverty line had comfortable living conditions. They lacked enough money to meet some of their basic needs, such as nutritious food and adequate clothing. But their homes had sufficient living space with air conditioning, refrigerators, stoves, microwaves, washers, dryers, and televisions. Most had cell phones, computers, and cars. Did this mean they were not poor?

The results of the survey sparked controversy. Many people argued that government handouts had allowed poor people luxuries they had not worked for and would not otherwise have been able to afford. They believed government spending on welfare—financial support for those in need—should be cut. Others pointed out that items such as cell phones, refrigerators, and stoves are necessities, not luxuries.

HARRINGTON'S *THE OTHER AMERICA*

Fifty years ago, Michael Harrington changed Americans' view of society. At a time when people believed most Americans were part of the comfortable middle class, *The Other America* showed nearly one-third of the population lived in poverty. In 1999, *Time* magazine listed *The Other America* among the top ten most influential nonfiction books of the 1900s. Harrington's work is credited as a spark that helped ignite the war on poverty. Harrington, however, placed the responsibility on US society. He said, "The fate of the poor hangs upon the decision of the better-off. If this anger and shame are not forthcoming, someone can write a book about the other America a generation from now and it will be the same or worse."[6]

Technology had made many items more affordable than in the past.

The Fight for $15 sparked further controversy over the consequences of raising the minimum wage. Some people argued that a dramatic increase in the minimum wage would force some businesses to close. Others insisted the increase in wages would enable hourly workers to provide for themselves and their families.

Would a federal requirement of paying workers at least $15 an hour lift thousands of people out of poverty? In part, the answer depends on the definition of poverty.

DEFINING POVERTY

One definition of poverty is tied to income. People who do not earn enough money to provide for their basic needs live below the poverty threshold. The US Census Bureau uses income levels for determining poverty status. The levels vary according to the size of a family and the ages of family members.

At the end of the 1900s, many people argued that income was not an accurate measurement of poverty. They pointed out the poverty threshold was outdated.

In order to put money toward other necessities, some families live in small apartments, sharing beds and other living spaces.

Mollie Orshansky, a government employee, developed standards for measuring poverty in the 1960s. These standards were based on the cost of foods needed to feed a family. At that time, expenditures for food represented approximately one-third of a family's budget. Orshansky's work became the official US poverty measure. By 2014, the percentage of family income spent on food was less than 10 percent, but the standards for measuring poverty had not changed. To address this issue, the US Census Bureau developed a Supplemental Poverty Measure (SPM) in 2014.

To determine poverty levels, the SPM considered the cost of food, clothing, shelter, and utilities as well as differences in geographic locations. It also counted taxes and benefits from government programs when determining a family's income. The results of using SPM indicated an increase in overall poverty rates when measured different ways, especially for senior citizens, but a decrease in childhood poverty rates.

THE COST OF LIVING

A standard of living is a measure of the quality of life. It is based on an ability to fill some wants as well as meet basic needs. People who live in poverty have a lower standard of living than those who earn higher incomes.

Basic living expenses include rent or mortgage payments, clothing, and groceries. Utilities, such as electricity or gas and water, are necessities. Phone, cable, and Internet are common expenses. Transportation costs include bus or train

POVERTY STATISTICS

According to 2014 US Census Bureau statistics, American Indian, African American, Hispanic, and immigrant populations in the United States had higher poverty levels than white or Asian populations. Without regard to race or ethnicity, groups with the highest percentages of poverty were unemployed adults, single mothers, adults without a high school diploma, and adults with a disability. Among children age 18 and younger, 21 percent were poor. Among seniors older than age 65, the poverty rate was 10 percent. Poverty statistics indicated the percentage of people in poverty was generally higher in the South than in other US regions. Mississippi, Arkansas, Louisiana, Kentucky, Georgia, and New Mexico were listed among the states with the highest percentage of poor people. Urban and rural areas had high poverty rates, but suburbs had the fastest growing percentage of poor residents.

2016 POVERTY GUIDELINES

NUMBER OF PEOPLE IN HOUSEHOLD	POVERTY LINE ANNUAL INCOME[7]
1	$11,880
2	$16,020
3	$20,160
4	$24,300
5	$28,440
6	$32,580
7	$36,730
8	$40,890

fare. Having a car involves payments, maintenance, gas, and insurance. Health care is a necessary expense, and childcare is needed when parents work. Federal income tax, property tax for homeowners, and state income tax in many places must also be considered in monthly budgets. These basic living expenses do not include extras such as entertainment or gifts, and they do not provide savings for the future or for unexpected expenses.

Living expenses vary greatly by location. A median family budget in the United States was approximately $63,000 for a household with two parents and two children in 2014.[8] The median budget indicated that half the households in the country had budgets higher than $63,000, and the other half had budgets lower than $63,000. According to a national survey that year, most families said they could "get by" on $58,000 a year.[9]

At a minimum wage of $7.25 per hour, a full-time employee earns approximately $15,000 a year before taxes. At a minimum

MINIMUM WAGE

The first federal minimum wage, introduced by President Franklin Roosevelt in 1938, was 25 cents an hour. In today's money, that would be approximately $4 an hour. Since 1938, the minimum wage has been raised 22 times. The last time was in 2009, when it was raised from $6.55 to $7.25.

wage of $15.00 per hour, a full-time employee would earn $31,000 a year before taxes. If poverty is defined by income alone, a minimum hourly wage of $15.00 would be the solution for many working people. However, the picture changes dramatically if poverty is defined by the amount people must spend on living expenses.

COST OF LIVING COMPARISON

The income needed to live comfortably, but modestly, varies from one part of the United States to another. In 2014, studies indicated a two-parent, two-child family required an annual income of $106,000 to live in Washington, DC. The same family could live comfortably in Morristown, Tennessee, for $49,000 a year. The differences are largely due to the costs of housing and childcare. For example, the monthly cost of housing for a family of four ranged from $1,956 in San Francisco, California, to $561 in some parts of Arkansas.[10] In most of the areas studied in 2014, childcare for two children was more expensive than rent.

MEASURING POVERTY

Statistics show poverty is widespread, and it affects almost all parts of the population. Some believe government programs are necessary to help people rise above the poverty line and become self-sufficient. Others argue government handouts have made the problems worse. To prevent poverty, it is necessary to understand its causes. To cure poverty, it is necessary to understand its consequences.

CHAPTER TWO

CAUSES OF POVERTY

Based on US Census Bureau data, approximately 15 percent of the US population in 2014 was poor. Indeed, the overall poverty rate had not changed significantly in four consecutive years. But for some groups—people with a college degree and married couples—the number had increased slightly. In a land of plenty, why are so many people poor? In some cases, the causes and the consequences of poverty are the same, which creates a perpetual cycle of poverty.

CAUSES OF POVERTY

The reasons why people lack money to meet their basic needs are complicated. Some people are too young or too old to work. Others have physical or

A mother chooses clothing from a donation center in Detroit, Michigan, after losing her job and home.

mental disabilities that prevent them from earning a living. These people rely on charity or welfare from government programs.

Many poor people are able and willing to work, but they lack job opportunities because they are uneducated or unskilled. The low-paying jobs available to them do not provide enough money for the education or training that would enable them to get better jobs. Even people working two or more minimum-wage jobs to support their families have a hard time escaping the cycle of poverty.

Critics of government assistance blame the system for causing poverty. They claim handouts from the government have provided people with an excuse to remain unemployed and unproductive. They believe these people choose to remain in poverty because they are lazy, alcoholics, or addicted to drugs.

Some people are born and raised in poverty. Statistics show that children raised by single mothers have a higher rate of poverty than other groups. In 2014, families headed by a single mother had a poverty rate of 30.6 percent, compared with 6.2 percent of married couple families.[1] Many single mothers can work only part time at

Raising children is an expensive task, especially for single parents.

low-paying jobs that fit around raising their children. The costs of childcare and transportation are beyond their budgets. As a result, children lack adequate nutrition, health care, and education. The cycle of poverty continues because these children become adults who do not have the skills to secure higher-paying jobs that would lift them out of poverty.

FALLING INTO POVERTY

While many people are born into poverty, others fall into poverty. This includes well-educated, skilled workers who lose their jobs for a variety of reasons. Businesses may close. Companies begin outsourcing work to overseas suppliers and eliminating jobs to cut costs. Improved technology enables companies to produce more work with fewer employees. Often these workers are overqualified for low-paying jobs, so they may remain unemployed and eventually fall below the poverty level.

THE POOREST CITY IN THE UNITED STATES

In the early 1900s, Detroit, Michigan, was the thriving center of the automobile industry. But in 2014, Detroit became the poorest large city in the United States. The decline in manufacturing jobs left many people unemployed and unable to afford basic needs. The city shut off water to thousands of residents who could not pay their water bills. According to 2015 Census Bureau figures, almost 40 percent of people in Detroit lived in poverty.

Medical expenses also push people into poverty. According to a 2011 US Census Bureau report, rising health-care costs were one of the highest living expenses for families. When out-of-pocket medical expenses—those not covered by health insurance—were considered, the poverty rate increased by approximately ten million people. Older adults, who tend to have fixed incomes and more health problems, were especially impacted by medical costs.

IMPACT OF ECONOMIC RECESSION

The US economic recession, which lasted from December 2007 to June 2009, caused a rise in the number of people in poverty. The collapse of the housing market resulted in a loss of wealth, cutbacks in spending, and massive job loss. Members of the middle class, who had enjoyed a comfortable life that included a home and a well-paying job, found themselves below the poverty line.

Darlena Cunha, a journalist in Boston, shared a typical story about her fall into poverty. She and her husband earned a combined income of $120,000 a year. When Cunha was pregnant with twins, the couple bought a home. Then her husband lost his job, and the twins were born prematurely. The mortgage payments and

SUBURBAN POVERTY

During the 1970s, most of the nation's poor lived in rural areas. A dramatic shift happened over the next three decades. During the 1980s and 1990s, poor populations increased in cities and surrounding areas. Then, between 2000 and 2010, the number of poor people in suburbs increased by twice as much as those living in cities. By 2010, the suburbs were home to the largest and fastest-growing poor population in the United States. One challenge faced by the suburban poor is the distance between affordable housing and job opportunities. Many workers spend considerable time and money commuting to their jobs. In a study of large metropolitan areas, low-income households spent almost as much on transportation as housing.

hospital bills strained their budget and exhausted their savings. Due to the housing crisis, their home lost value. They went underwater on the mortgage, which meant the house was not worth what they owed on it. At the same time, their income had decreased to $25,000 a year. This once-successful couple learned firsthand what it was like to rely on government aid for food.

Older workers were hit especially hard by the recession. Those who lost their jobs had less chance of finding work than some of their younger coworkers. Those who were planning to retire had to postpone their retirement and build up their savings. Those who had retired suffered loss of savings and investments, and the value of their homes decreased.

The impact of the recession lasted long after the economy began to recover. The Center on Budget and Policy Procedures indicated that effects were still being felt in the first quarter of 2016. Many middle-class families continued to struggle—often working more than one job—to rise above the poverty level.

CONSEQUENCES OF POVERTY

According to a study by the Urban Institute in 2013, living in deep poverty—less than $6,000 a year for one adult—has many serious consequences. These include continuing health problems, depression, addiction, and homelessness. People living in deep poverty may be overweight or obese because they eat foods that are cheap and available rather than foods that provide good nutrition.

Disability is a cause and a consequence of poverty. People in deep poverty often have physical disabilities because they live in an unhealthy environment, and they have limited access to health care. People with physical disabilities often cannot work. The poverty

HOMELESSNESS

Between 2007 and 2008, the number of homeless families in the United States increased substantially. The increases were generally linked to the economic recession beginning in 2007. Millions of people lost their homes because they could not afford to make mortgage payments. This increased the number of people seeking affordable places to rent. A survey in 2011 showed an increase in homeless populations in 55 percent of the communities studied.[2] By 2014, some cities still reported increases, but overall homelessness had decreased. Even so, during a one-night national survey in January 2014, more than 500,000 people in the United States were sleeping on the streets, in cars, in emergency shelters, or in temporary housing.[3] According to the Department of Housing and Urban Development in 2014, the country needed at least seven million more affordable apartments for low-income families.

rate for people with disabilities is more than twice as high as that for people without disabilities.

In 2014, more than 16 million children in the United States lived in poverty.[4] Approximately seven million of those children lived in deep poverty.[5] Poor children have a high risk of physical and mental health problems. Research indicates the stress of living in poverty from

The millions of children living in poverty rely on benefits such as free meals at school since their families usually cannot provide enough.

birth to age two can harm brain development and put a child at risk for future health problems.

Other consequences of poverty extend to the future. Because public schools are funded by local property taxes, schools in poor neighborhoods lack resources to provide quality education. Poor children are less likely to succeed in school or in life.

Of children who are born in deep poverty, 14 percent will remain deeply poor until the age of 40.[6] The chances of their becoming productive citizens are decreased by their lack of opportunity. Approximately 29 percent of adults without a high school diploma live in poverty.[7]

IMPACT OF CHILDHOOD POVERTY AND HOMELESSNESS

In a 2014 survey, school districts reported more than one million homeless children in public schools. Homelessness resulted in poor school performance, the need to repeat a grade, and reduced graduation rates. For some children, homelessness is a temporary situation, but poverty may be long-term. Lack of proper nutrition and health care can result in infant death, frequent and severe diseases, poor growth and development, and increased complications due to being overweight. Children who are raised in poverty from a young age often have difficulty in school. Until recently, poor academic performance was blamed on such factors as stress, lack of confidence, or lack of experiences. Recent research discovered that childhood poverty affects brain development. Poor children may experience problems with memory, emotions, and speech. Fortunately, researchers found the negative effects of poverty on brain development can be reduced through supportive caregiving.

"WE SHOULD HAVE NO POOR CHILDREN IN THE RICHEST NATION ON EARTH. . . . WE DON'T HAVE A MONEY PROBLEM. WE HAVE A PROFOUND VALUES AND PRIORITIES PROBLEM."[9]

— MARIAN WRIGHT EDELMAN, PRESIDENT OF CHILDREN'S DEFENSE FUND, TESTIFYING BEFORE CONGRESS ON APRIL 30, 2014

As life expectancy increases, so does the percentage of older people living in poverty. Failing health and rising medical costs cause people to fall below the poverty line. The overall poverty rate of 10 percent for people 65 and older is lower than that of other age groups. This is due largely to Social Security. In 2014, almost half of single adults age 65 and over depended on Social Security for 90 percent of their income.[8]

Three-quarters of deeply poor adults surveyed in 2013 had been out of work for one year or more. Their ability to find a job was limited by lack of education, transportation, or childcare; criminal record; or poor health. Their lack of opportunity to support themselves and their families leads to other problems.

CAN THE PROBLEM BE FIXED?

Improved educational opportunities for children may help lead to a solution for escaping the cycle of poverty.

MORE TO THE STORY

NOT GETTING BY IN THE UNITED STATES

Poverty is not limited to one age group, one location, or one race or ethnicity. The stories of Jairo Gomez and Victoria Brownworth illustrate differences and similarities among the invisible poor. Jairo Gomez is a teenager who lives in a one-bedroom apartment with his mother, stepfather, and six siblings in New York City. With an annual income of $30,000, the Gomez family is $15,000 below the poverty line. In order to make it possible for their mom to work as a cleaning lady, the oldest children stay home from school to take care of the younger ones. Jairo works at a low-paying job to earn money to move out. But his education has suffered, and without a diploma, he has little chance of success.

Victoria Brownworth was a successful journalist in Philadelphia when the recession hit in 2008. The newspapers she wrote for suffered cutbacks, and her income was cut in half. Brownworth became one of the working poor—a middle-aged, single woman with an education and an income that did not qualify her for government benefits. She wrote about her experiences to raise awareness that "America's poor . . . continue to walk among the rest of you, invisible as ever."[10]

"YOUNG PEOPLE CAN VIRTUALLY ASSURE THAT THEY AND THEIR FAMILIES WILL AVOID POVERTY IF THEY FOLLOW THREE ELEMENTARY RULES FOR SUCCESS—COMPLETE AT LEAST A HIGH SCHOOL EDUCATION, WORK FULL TIME, AND WAIT UNTIL AGE 21 AND GET MARRIED BEFORE HAVING A BABY."[11]

— RON HASKINS OF THE BROOKINGS INSTITUTION, TESTIFYING BEFORE CONGRESS ON JUNE 5, 2012

Research shows a strong connection between quality early childhood education and successful child development. A person with a high school diploma has a better chance of getting a job and earning a higher annual income than someone without a high school education.

An opportunity to receive job training would seem to be another solution to the problem of poverty. For people without a high school diploma, basic education classes provide an opportunity to improve reading and math skills, which could lead to better jobs.

Some past government aid programs required people to participate in education or training before they could receive benefits. This strategy had mixed results. Although education and training improved the quality of the workers, they did not improve the quality or number of jobs available. Another approach to moving people off welfare focused on getting a job. The goal was to help people find jobs, even low-paying jobs, as a way of building skills. The skills included resume-writing and interviewing, as well as on-the-job training that could lead to higher pay. In the meantime, however, low-paying jobs did not lift people out of poverty, and one-quarter of the jobs in the United States still pay below the poverty line.

Two unemployed veterans study together in Texas in the hopes of finding a job.

DECLARING WAR ON POVERTY

In 1963, President John F. Kennedy began planning measures to help the one-fifth of the population that was in poverty at the time. But it was his successor, Lyndon B. Johnson, who carried out the plan. Just a few weeks after Kennedy's assassination, in his State of the Union address on January 8, 1964, President Johnson asked Congress and the American people to join him in "working for a nation that is free from want."[1]

Johnson outlined his vision for a better United States during a commencement speech at the University of Michigan in May 1964. He challenged the graduating class to help build a Great Society in which every citizen could have full equality and an escape from poverty. The Great Society was a set of

President Lyndon B. Johnson delivered his State of the Union address in 1964 and called for changes to address poverty.

programs aimed at improving the environment, increasing educational opportunities, and eliminating poverty in the United States.

A DECLARATION OF WAR

Between 1964 and 1968, Johnson's War on Poverty consisted of 200 pieces of legislation proposed by the administration, passed by Congress, and carried out by federal, state, and local government agencies, as well as numerous community-based nonprofit organizations. With a budget of $1 billion, Johnson's policies were the largest expansion of government assistance programs in history. The War on Poverty became a cornerstone of Johnson's Great Society. The four major parts of the program were the Social Security Act Amendments, the Food Stamp Act, the Economic Opportunity Act, and the Elementary and Secondary Education Act.

"POVERTY IS A NATIONAL PROBLEM, REQUIRING IMPROVED NATIONAL ORGANIZATION AND SUPPORT. BUT THIS ATTACK, TO BE EFFECTIVE, MUST ALSO BE ORGANIZED AT THE STATE AND THE LOCAL LEVEL AND MUST BE SUPPORTED AND DIRECTED BY STATE AND LOCAL EFFORTS."[2]

— PRESIDENT LYNDON JOHNSON, 1964

The Social Security Amendments of the 1960s

People line up to receive food stamps in Baltimore, Maryland, in the 1970s.

expanded the benefits of Social Security, which had been started by President Franklin Roosevelt in the 1930s. These amendments created Medicare to provide medical coverage for retirees. They also created Medicaid to provide access to health-care benefits for families and individuals with low incomes and limited resources. Social Security benefits were increased and expanded to provide financial assistance for widows and the disabled. The Food Stamp Act created a permanent program to provide low-income people with stamps they could exchange for food in grocery stores.

The Economic Opportunity Act created the Job Corps to provide job training and opportunities for young, poor people. The centerpiece was the Community Action Program, designed to encourage "maximum feasible participation" of the poor through local community action agencies that would design and execute a comprehensive, coordinated approach to reducing poverty.[3] The Elementary and Secondary Education Act created Title I to provide financial aid to school districts demonstrating high rates of poverty in order to expand and improve their educational programs.

SARGENT SHRIVER

Sargent Shriver worked in both the Kennedy and Johnson administrations and was noted for his lifetime of service to his country. As leader of the War on Poverty, he launched its most notable programs. Shriver's goal was empowering poor people to help themselves. Once asked which of the antipoverty programs he thought was most important, Shriver chose Legal Services. The program enabled poor people to gain access to lawyers who would represent them and help them gain rights and benefits through legal action. Legal Services was part of Shriver's goal to "weave . . . patterns of justice, opportunity, dignity, and mutual respect."[4]

CARRYING OUT THE WAR ON POVERTY

The Economic Opportunity Act also established the Office of Economic Opportunity (OEO) to carry out the War on Poverty programs. President Johnson appointed Sargent Shriver as head of the OEO and director of the War on Poverty. Under Shriver's leadership, the OEO created community action agencies to carry out antipoverty programs. These agencies were required to have local residents, especially low-income residents, on their boards. In this way, the US government urged needy citizens to organize to help themselves.

"THE SIMPLEST DESCRIPTION OF THE WAR ON POVERTY IS THAT IT IS A MEANS OF MAKING LIFE AVAILABLE FOR ANY AND ALL PURSUERS. . . . THE WAR ON POVERTY TRIES ONLY TO CREATE THE CONDITIONS BY WHICH THE GOOD LIFE CAN BE LIVED."[5]

— SARGENT SHRIVER, 1964

Johnson's plan involved a cooperative effort with state and local governments to carry out national programs. Key programs targeted specific groups of society. Head Start, for example, promoted school readiness for young children. Job Corps provided free education and job training for men and women ages 16 to 24. Medicare provided health-care coverage for people older than 65. The Community Action Program supported a wide range of programs and services to assist poor people and poor neighborhoods.

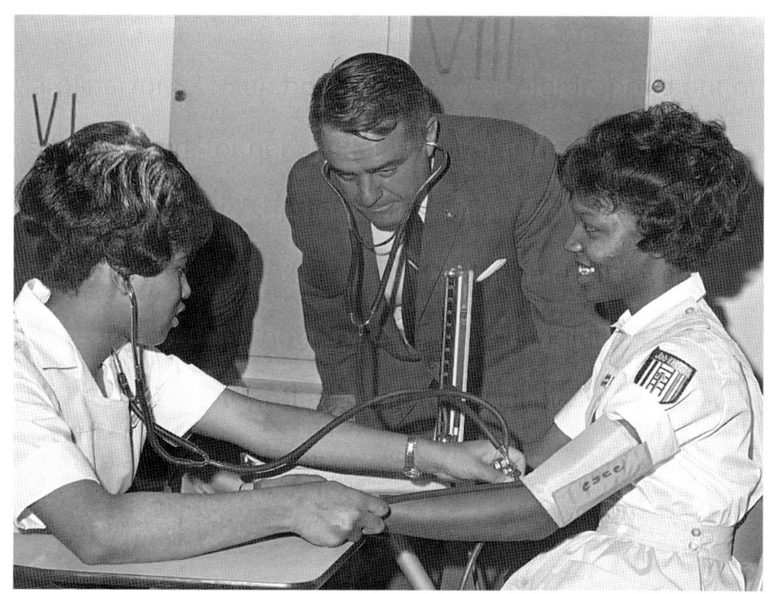

Shriver's work gave the poor opportunities that could help them out of poverty.

In 1961, President Kennedy had established the Peace Corps. This group of volunteers travels overseas to provide health care, education, and other services to communities in need. Kennedy also had proposed a national service corps to perform similar services in the United States. In 1965, President Johnson carried out that plan by establishing Volunteers in Service to America (VISTA) to serve the needs of the poor in urban and rural areas. Within a few years, VISTA volunteers developed a variety of projects throughout the country. Their work helped start small businesses, farm cooperatives, and credit unions in poor communities.

POVERTY AND CIVIL RIGHTS

> "SHRIVER MAY HAVE HELPED MORE PEOPLE AROUND THE WORLD THAN ANY TWENTIETH CENTURY AMERICAN WHO WASN'T A PRESIDENT, POLITICIAN, OR MARTIN LUTHER KING."[6]
>
> **— SCOTT STOSSEL, SARGENT SHRIVER BIOGRAPHER**

Civil rights, like poverty, was a priority of Johnson's administration. In some ways, the two concerns overlapped. Civil rights leader Dr. Martin Luther King Jr. recognized this. Shortly before his assassination in 1968, King was working on the Poor People's Campaign, which he hoped would focus the attention of Congress and the American people on the problem of poverty.

King intended to include people of all races, not just black people, in his fight for jobs with fair wages, better education, and unemployment benefits. Part of the plan was to build a tent city in Washington, DC, to bring the problems of the poor to the doorstep of the nation's leaders. King proposed the government take a direct approach to the problems by providing everyone with a guaranteed income. King died before he could launch the Poor People's Campaign, but the fight against poverty continued.

FROM THE HEADLINES

APPALACHIAN POVERTY

Appalachia is a region that extends through 13 states, from southern New York to northern Mississippi. It is known for both its natural beauty and its extreme poverty. During the 1960s, Appalachia became a focus of the War on Poverty. Kennedy visited West Virginia during the 1960 presidential campaign. His direct contact with the region's depressed economic conditions brought public attention to the issues and influenced policies of his administration. In 1965, Lyndon B. Johnson signed legislation that would "bring impoverished areas of Appalachia into the mainstream American economy."[7]

Residents of Appalachia viewed the results of Johnson's legislation in different ways. Patsy Dowling grew up in North Carolina in the 1960s. She credited Head Start with helping her and her classmates overcome their families' financial difficulties. But other Appalachia residents disliked the unwelcome attention and stereotypes that resulted from the media focus. Some residents felt politicians used the region to further their own careers or gain votes. The residents viewed the portrayal of Appalachia as one-sided and unfair.

The Appalachian Regional Commission (ARC) was designed to promote development of the region through investments in infrastructure, social programs, and regional planning and coordination. One study found the ARC counties grew faster in

President Johnson talks with a father of eight children living in poverty in Appalachia.

terms of population and income than did comparable counties in other parts of the country between 1969 and 1991. A subsequent report confirmed these findings over the ARC's first 50 years. According to ARC, the number of high-poverty counties declined from 295 in 1960 to 107 in 2012, and the overall poverty rate of the region dropped from more than 30 percent in 1960 to less than 17 percent in 2012.

GUARANTEED INCOME

Martin Luther King Jr.'s idea of guaranteed income was based on a belief that a direct approach to ending poverty was needed. He criticized the indirect programs that tried to solve poverty by first solving something else. Rather than providing better housing or education, King believed the government should provide every household with a sum of money to spend each year. According to King's plan, the guaranteed income would raise people out of poverty and into the middle class. The amount would increase as necessary to keep up with the middle class standard of living. Although the idea may seem radical today, in the late 1960s, some viewed it as a possible alternative to the welfare system.

LEGACY OF THE WAR ON POVERTY

By 1968, the Vietnam War (1954–1975) began to overshadow the War on Poverty. Funds that had been used to fight poverty at home were needed to fight the war. In many ways, the unpopularity of the Vietnam War overshadowed the achievements of Johnson's programs to improve life for Americans at home.

Although the success or failure of the War on Poverty is greatly debated, poverty decreased between 1963, when Johnson took office, and 1970, when the impact of his programs was assessed. During that time, the number of Americans living in poverty dropped from 22.2 percent to 12.6 percent of the population.[8] Some attribute the decline to government action. Others argue the trend was already in place before the War on Poverty began.

The OEO was eventually replaced by other agencies. But many of the programs it created still existed more than 50 years later. The programs and local agencies created by the War on Poverty continue to play an important role in coordinating programs and services for the poor in communities of all types.

Many have contested the benefits of government programs to aid the poor. However, studies show that the US safety net cuts poverty in half. Federal, state, and local governments, as well as private, philanthropic organizations continue to play a role in providing aid to people in need. The challenge today, as it was during the War on Poverty, is how to foster a concentrated, coordinated, community-based approach to fighting poverty.

IMPACT OF THE VIETNAM WAR

The Vietnam War was a conflict aimed at stopping the spread of communism in Southeast Asia. It began before Johnson became president, but US military involvement increased dramatically during his administration. Johnson sent US combat forces into battle in March 1965. As US involvement in the war increased, so did the costs. The US economy strained to support the war as well as the War on Poverty programs. Reports of US casualties grew, and so did antiwar sentiment. Johnson's approval ratings dropped. He no longer had the necessary support from Congress to maintain his War on Poverty programs.

CHAPTER FOUR

PROGRAMS FOR THE POOR

Many of the programs that started during Johnson's administration have continued to the present. Others have been updated or replaced with new ways of providing benefits to individuals and families. These include contributory programs, such as Social Security, Medicare, and Unemployment Compensation. Contributory programs are available to all Americans who have contributed to them through taxes, regardless of income level.

Welfare programs, sometimes called the safety net, provide help to low-income Americans. These are means-tested programs, available only to individuals whose income is below a certain level. They are free to

Social Security is one of the programs created by Johnson that has lasted for decades.

SECURITY
SOCIAL SEC
SECURIT
SOCIAL S

anyone whose income level qualifies for the benefits, but qualifications vary for each program.

FEDERAL SAFETY NET

Federal welfare programs are funded mostly by tax dollars and are administered by different federal government agencies. Each program has its own rules, and it focuses on a specific aspect of poverty. The purpose of the federal safety net is to provide for the basic needs of people who are living in poverty and help lift them above the poverty level.

The federal safety net consists of 13 categories of programs that provide cash, food, housing, job training, and education for people who qualify. It also includes Medicaid, which represents the largest spending of all the antipoverty programs. Each state decides what its Medicaid program will cover and who is eligible for benefits, but states must also follow federal guidelines.

Tax credits are the next largest category of government welfare spending. The two programs are the Earned Income Tax Credit (EITC) and the Child Tax Credit (CTC). These programs reduce the amount of tax owed by

A Medicaid recipient gets help from his caregiver in the comfort of his home.

low-income workers. The EITC is available to individuals or families based on income. Low-income workers who do not owe income tax, or whose tax is lowered to zero because of their tax credit for the year, receive the EITC as a payment. The CTC provides an additional credit for taxpayers with dependent children under the age of 17.

After Medicaid and tax credit programs, the Supplemental Nutrition Assistance Program (SNAP) is the largest government welfare expense. SNAP provides additional funds to help people buy healthful foods. The funds are based on US Department of Agriculture estimates of how much it costs to buy nutritious food for low-cost meals. The benefits people receive depend upon the size of their households. People who qualify for benefits receive an electronic transfer card, which is similar to a debit card, linked to an account. They can use the card to help pay for groceries.

A fourth major category of government spending on welfare is Supplemental Security Income (SSI). This program provides payments to people older than 65, as well as those of any age, who are blind or disabled, including children. In 2015, Medicaid, tax credits, SNAP, and SSI accounted for more than three-quarters of government spending to aid people living in poverty.

THE SNAP CHALLENGE

In 2016, the average monthly SNAP benefit per person was $126.37. That is approximately $4.21 per day, or $1.40 per meal. The SNAP challenge, supported by the Food Research and Action Center (FRAC), encouraged people not living in poverty to experience what life was like for the millions of Americans whose food budget was limited to less than $5.00 per day. Many people, including high-profile celebrities and members of Congress, accepted the challenge. In addition to raising awareness of the problem of hunger in the United States, the SNAP challenge provided other insights. Participants discovered the challenge of eating a healthful diet when fresh fruits and vegetables generally exceeded the budget. They also experienced the effects of hunger and poor nutrition, such as tiredness and difficulty concentrating. According to FRAC, people who took part in the SNAP challenge came away with a greater understanding of this aspect of poverty and became antihunger advocates.

OTHER SAFETY NET PROGRAMS

CHILD NUTRITION	Provides needy children with school breakfast, lunch, and after-school food programs
HEAD START	Provides preschool programs
HOUSING ASSISTANCE	Provides rental assistance or access to low-cost housing to keep housing costs to 30 percent of income
LIFELINE	Provides help with home or cell phone costs
LOW INCOME HOME ENERGY ASSISTANCE PROGRAM	Provides assistance to needy families to pay for heating or cooling their homes
PELL GRANTS	Provides assistance with college expenses for low-income students
TEMPORARY ASSISTANCE FOR NEEDY FAMILIES (TANF)	Provides assistance to needy families through state-run programs
WOMEN, INFANTS, AND CHILDREN (WIC)	Provides high-protein food for pregnant women and children up to five years old

STATES' RESPONSIBILITY FOR SAFETY NET PROGRAMS

In 1996, Congress created the Temporary Assistance for Needy Families (TANF) program, which changed the way public assistance was provided to needy families. First, it imposed a five-year lifetime limit on federal welfare assistance. Second, it imposed a work requirement, requiring adults without disabilities to be engaged in work or a work activity as a condition of receiving TANF assistance.

TANF REQUIREMENTS

One key feature of TANF is the requirement that people must be involved in work-related activities in order to receive benefits. The requirement does not apply to people who are mentally or physically unable to work. Other reasons for not working include lack of childcare for young children. Most adults must work a certain number of hours per week, based on federal guidelines. For example, a single parent must be involved in work activities 30 hours a week. For two-parent families, the work requirements are 35 to 55 hours per week.

TANF gave states greater power over the design of their welfare programs and increased flexibility over the use of federal funds. Each state can design its own programs and determine the requirements and payments for participants. Benefit payments to needy families range from $200 to $900 a month, depending upon the state in which they live. States determine who gets funds, and they can shorten the five-year federal time limit for cash assistance available to families. Based on federal guidelines, states can also extend assistance beyond five years for reasons of hardship.

Because states can shift TANF funds to other purposes, many people feel the safety net for the nation's poorest families has been weakened. In 2014, states used only approximately 26 percent of TANF funds as cash payments to meet needy families' basic needs.[1] Most of the funds were used for other services, including work-related activities, childcare, and educational programs.

STATES TAKE ACTION

Since 2003, a number of state governments have taken action to fight poverty. They have established commissions or special task forces to study the problems of the poor and develop strategies for solving them. Many of the states set concrete goals, such as cutting the poverty rate in half within a decade. Policy recommendations vary by state, but most include ways to expand access to existing aid, such as federal and state tax credits, food assistance programs, and childcare. Other strategies address job training and employment as well as access to transportation systems. The focused attention of a state task force was considered an important step in creating policy changes to reduce poverty.

LOCAL PROGRAMS

Federal agencies often partner with local communities to deliver aid to needy individuals and families. The Office of Community Services, for example, is an agency of the US Department of Health and Human Services. It works with states and communities to reduce the causes of poverty and to improve the lives of people in need.

Thousands of nonprofit groups and faith-based charities also serve the needs of the poor in communities throughout the nation. Many of these services started as one person's idea and grew into a much larger network of aid. In the late 1960s, John van Hengel, a retired businessman, established a food bank in Phoenix, Arizona. Food from grocery stores and other sources in the food industry, which would otherwise be thrown away, was stored and distributed to people in need. Today, Feeding America is a national organization with more than 200 food banks that provide groceries to 46 million people through hundreds of local food pantries.

"THE MONTH IS LONGER THAN THE MONEY."[2]

— BILLYE MCPHERSON, 84-YEAR-OLD WOMAN EXPLAINING WHY SHE RAN A FOOD PANTRY IN CALIFORNIA

MORE TO THE STORY

THE ALICE PROJECT

The United Way is a nonprofit organization that partners with communities to help poor people escape poverty. Its Asset Limited, Income Constrained, Employed (ALICE) Project program began in New Jersey in 2009. It is an effort to improve the lives of the people who work hard and earn more than the federal poverty level, but cannot afford housing, childcare, food, transportation, and health care. Since 2009, the ALICE Project has spread to 15 states.

With the support of large corporations and through extensive media coverage and social media attention, ALICE has gained public interest. The project has generated research into better ways of helping low-income families. For example, United Parcel Service (UPS) recognized that many military veterans were among the working poor and committed to hiring 50,000 veterans. The ALICE Project focuses attention on a group that is often overlooked. Through community action, it works to help struggling families become self-sufficient.

SHELTERING THE HOMELESS

Public Action to Deliver Shelter (PADS) began in DuPage County, Illinois, in 1985 with one site that provided overnight shelter for homeless people. By 2015, PADS operated at 31 sites, 365 nights a year, staffed by volunteers from local churches and other organizations. Each site provides overnight shelter, breakfast, dinner, and a bag lunch. Many sites provide showers and laundry facilities. In addition, PADS expanded its services with a goal of helping people become self-sufficient. It provides employment support, aids people in finding permanent housing, and connects people with medical services. The PADS slogan, "When someone believes in you, everything can change," became a model for other communities to follow in working toward an end to homelessness.[3]

Thousands of local soup kitchens, which provide free meals, and homeless shelters, which provide a safe, clean place to sleep, operate in communities throughout the country. These places provide necessary and useful services for the poor, but they do not solve the problem of poverty. Addressing the causes of poverty and finding ways to lift people out of poverty have been the focus of political debate for generations.

Most soup kitchens are funded through donations and staffed by volunteers.

CHAPTER FIVE

POLITICS AND POVERTY

In January 2016, several Republican presidential candidates gathered in South Carolina for a discussion about the issues surrounding poverty in the United States. The meeting, hosted by Senator Tim Scott and House Speaker Paul Ryan, was unusual in a campaign in which policy discussions had been rare.

The seven candidates who took part in the discussion differed in their proposed solutions to the problem of poverty. But they generally agreed on the need for Republicans to reach out to the percent of the population living in poverty—a group that had traditionally supported Democrats. The meeting in South Carolina, and the 2016 campaign in general,

President Barack Obama volunteered at an organization that helps people living in poverty.

Martha's Table
EDUCATION · FOOD · OPPORTUNITY

highlighted the connection between politics and poverty.

GUARANTEED ANNUAL INCOME

Instead of maintaining numerous federal welfare programs, why not give people money directly? That was the thinking behind a guaranteed annual income. The Family Assistance Plan, created by President Nixon in 1969, proposed replacing other programs with a cash payment of $1,600 to those in need. Others have proposed similar ideas. One plan suggested eliminating all welfare programs, including Social Security and Medicare, and giving an annual cash payment of $10,000 to everyone 21 years and older. Depending on the size and scope of guaranteed income programs, these programs could cost more than current government welfare spending and therefore require an increase in taxes. The strongest objection, however, is that doling out cash payments would destroy the incentive to work and achieve self-sufficiency that has been the goal of welfare for decades.

PRESIDENTS AND POVERTY

In 1964, President Johnson declared a War on Poverty and established policies that many consider the largest expansion of federal safety net programs in history. Since then, other presidents have made changes to the welfare system. Richard Nixon strongly opposed some of Johnson's programs, but he expanded Social Security, the food stamp program, and housing assistance. Gerald Ford signed the EITC, which some believe became the federal government's most cost-effective antipoverty program. This tax credit provides benefits to working people with children.

Low income New Yorkers receive free tax help as part of the EITC program.

In his 1988 State of the Union address, Ronald Reagan said, "Some years ago, the Federal Government declared war on poverty, and poverty won."[1] Although Reagan was a strong opponent of welfare, he expanded the EITC as part of a larger tax reform act.

Bill Clinton signed the Personal Responsibility and Work Opportunity Reconciliation Act in 1996. The law changed the government safety net for the poor into a system that required work in exchange for benefits, which could be received for a limited amount of time. The Clinton administration also created the Empowerment Zones and Enterprise Communities initiative. This effort fosters the creation of community-based strategies to increase economic opportunity and sustainable community development in high-poverty neighborhoods. The Clinton administration dramatically expanded the Federal HOPE VI program, which transforms distressed public housing projects in many cities into vibrant mixed-income, mixed-use communities with greater access to opportunities for low- and moderate-income families and children.

"FROM NOW ON, OUR NATION'S ANSWER TO THIS GREAT SOCIAL CHALLENGE WILL NO LONGER BE A NEVER-ENDING CYCLE OF WELFARE. IT WILL BE THE DIGNITY, THE POWER, AND THE ETHIC OF WORK."[2]

— PRESIDENT BILL CLINTON, REGARDING THE PERSONAL RESPONSIBILITY AND WORK OPPORTUNITY RECONCILIATION ACT, 1996

The policies of presidents Bill Clinton and George W. Bush expanded health-care programs for children and seniors. But the most sweeping change in health-care benefits for low-income people was Barack Obama's Affordable Care Act of 2010. The law expanded access to health insurance for those who were previously uninsured due to the high costs of coverage.

Presidential policies have tended to reflect political party philosophies. Democrats, such as Johnson

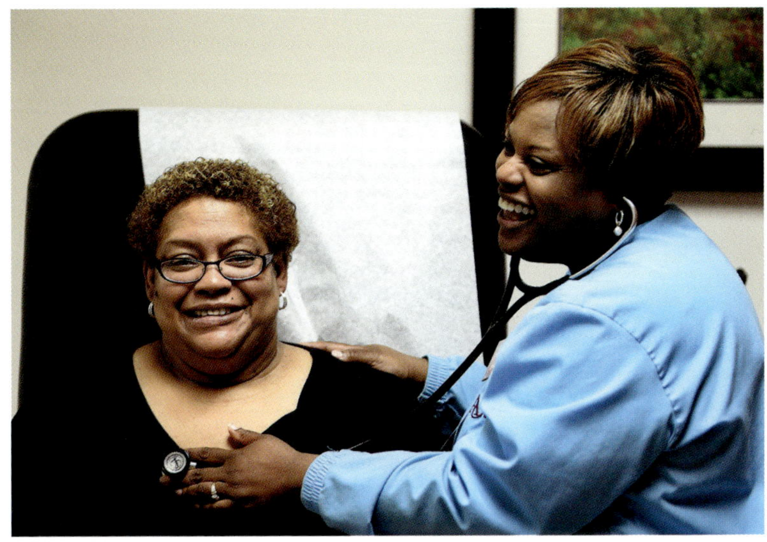

The Affordable Care Act made health insurance readily available to everyone despite their income.

and Obama, supported policies that involved more government. Republicans, such as Reagan and Bush, supported less government involvement and promoted stronger economic growth, which would benefit the poor.

GETTING OUT THE VOTE

Presidential politics is about winning votes. Both political parties recognize the value of gaining the support of the poor. But poor people generally do not vote. In the 2012 presidential election, 48 percent of eligible voters with family incomes of $20,000 or less voted. By comparison, 80 percent of eligible voters with family incomes of $150,000 or more voted in 2012.[3]

"THE BILL I'M SIGNING TODAY IS NOT ONLY AN HISTORIC OVERHAUL OF OUR TAX CODE AND A SWEEPING VICTORY FOR FAIRNESS, IT'S ALSO THE BEST ANTIPOVERTY BILL, THE BEST PRO-FAMILY MEASURE, AND THE BEST JOB-CREATION PROGRAM EVER TO COME OUT OF THE CONGRESS OF THE UNITED STATES."[5]

—PRESIDENT RONALD REAGAN AT THE SIGNING OF THE TAX REFORM ACT, 1986

Surveys of low-income voters indicate time and money are two barriers preventing people from going to the polls. Voter registration is low—only 8.9 million of the 14.3 million eligible low-income voters registered to vote in 2012.[4] Since low-income people often move between elections, few take the time to register in their new precinct. Elections are held on a weekday, which requires voters to take time off work and sometimes wait in line to vote. For hourly workers, time off means less pay.

The cost of transportation to the polls is a problem for some voters. Voter ID laws also pose a financial hardship. Several states require an ID that costs between $5.00 and $58.50. Most states offer a free ID for those who cannot afford the fee, but the documents required to prove identity, such as a birth certificate or a passport, also cost money.

Perhaps the strongest reason people living in poverty do not vote is they feel politicians have no understanding of their problems. Cassandra, a working mom once on welfare in Cincinnati, Ohio, recalled politicians who referred to people on welfare as lazy people who do not work. She realized the politicians knew very little about how she lived, and most of them did not seem to care. "We're not equal citizens," she said.[6]

WALKING IN THEIR SHOES

Although some politicians come from a poor background or have gained insights through working with the poor, most have no personal experience with poverty. In 2014, more than half the members of Congress were millionaires. The annual salary for senators and representatives was $174,000. The people in control of poverty programs, such as affordable housing, food assistance, and low-cost health care, lived nowhere near the poverty level. Writer Stephen Lurie observed, "Maybe the country would be better off if they had some firsthand encounters with need."[7]

Periodic attempts to walk in the shoes of the poor have made politicians more sensitive to the needs of

Those who live in poverty believe lawmakers do not fully understand the issues and problems people in poverty face.

those living in poverty. In 1987, Republican representative Stewart McKinney led the Great American Sleep Out to call attention to the plight of homeless people. The experience prompted other members of Congress to support McKinney's landmark legislation, which provided assistance to homeless Americans.

To protest Republican-proposed cuts to SNAP benefits in 2013, 26 Democrats in Congress volunteered to live on the SNAP food budget of approximately $1.40 per meal for a week. Participants reported the challenges of buying healthy food and the negative effects of hunger and poor diet on their well-being and ability to concentrate. Some Republicans criticized the experiment, claiming Democrats exaggerated the problems of those who receive SNAP benefits and indicating how a family could eat well on a SNAP budget. Legislation passed in 2014 cut nearly $9 billion dollars in SNAP benefits over a ten-year period.

LISTENING TO THEIR VOICES

In July 2014, Representative Paul Ryan held the fifth in a series of congressional budget committee hearings on poverty and the social safety net. Such meetings gather information that is used to influence spending on government programs. This meeting was different. A person actually living in poverty was invited to testify before the committee.

Tianna Gaines-Turner lived in Philadelphia, Pennsylvania, with her husband and three children. Both parents worked, but their combined income

EXPERIENCING HOMELESSNESS

On a single night in January 2015, approximately 565,000 people in the United States were homeless.[8] The Department of Housing and Urban Development requires communities to provide such counts in order to qualify for federal assistance. Some of the people sleep in homeless shelters, but others are on the streets. Reasons include lack of enough beds in shelters. People sometimes have to line up for hours in order to get space in a shelter. Those who work cannot get there in time. Other reasons include fear of theft and fear of contracting disease, bedbugs, or lice. Some homeless people prefer to risk freezing rather than suffer the conditions in some shelters. Events such as the Great American Sleep Out are held annually to raise awareness and earn money for the homeless. These events allow adults and teenagers to experience some of the discomfort of homelessness. But they can never duplicate what it truly means to be without a home.

was approximately $16,000 a year. Gaines-Turner gave a firsthand account of what it was like to live in poverty. Her family did not have health insurance, but medical care was needed for the children. If a parent had to take time off to care for a child, the family lost income. The SNAP benefit was not enough for a healthy diet.

Gaines-Turner fielded questions from the committee, including a comment from Representative Tom Rice: "If you rely on federal programs you'll never get out of poverty. The only way out of poverty is to be self-reliant and find yourself a job." Gaines-Turner had a job. She explained, "People living in poverty . . . want to create our own safety nets, so we never have to depend on government assistance again."[9]

VOICES OF THE POOR

Tianna Gaines-Turner proposed three ways for the government to solve poverty:

Provide living wages and labor practices that favor families. Give tax breaks to companies that offer stable employment and health benefits. Aid companies in providing paid sick leave and affordable, quality childcare.

Do not cut programs that keep people healthy. Improve the safety net to provide nutrition, housing assistance, education, and health care to families while they work to move themselves out of poverty.

Invest in community solutions. Include people who know poverty in making policy decisions. Gaines-Turner felt strongly that Congress should not make decisions about people living in poverty without talking to the people who know the issues firsthand. "If you do not have an understanding of the struggles," she asked, "how can you try to solve them?"[10]

MORE TO THE STORY

VOICES OF THE PAST

Efforts to incorporate voices of the poor into public policymaking began during Johnson's War on Poverty in the 1960s. Community Action Agencies were established as local organizations that empowered residents to take an active role in the design and administration of programs to aid the poor.

Since the 1960s, other federal poverty programs promoted participation by citizens. One example was Clinton's Empowerment Zones and Enterprise Communities. These programs provided federal funding for economic renewal and job creation in communities that qualified by geographic size, population, and poverty rate. The programs required participation by community-based partnerships of residents, businesses, local leaders, and community groups.

Since the 1990s, growing partnerships between low-income people and organizations has continued to work to address the issues of poverty within communities. Largely funded by national foundations, these efforts focus on community change. They engage residents in decision-making and in carrying out tasks, such as improving school readiness or increasing employment.

HAND UP OR HANDOUT?

In 1964, when Shriver became director of the OEO, President Johnson gave him one directive—"no doles." Johnson was strongly against the growth of a system that relied on welfare payments. He stated, "Our American answer to poverty is not to make the poor more secure in their poverty but to reach down and to help them lift themselves out of the ruts of poverty."[1]

The motto of the War on Poverty became "Hand up, not handouts." In the 50 years since the War on Poverty, people have continued to debate which term applies to government welfare programs.

A single mother signs up for food and services at a food pantry in Wheaton, Illinois.

PROS AND CONS

Proponents of the welfare system point out that federal government programs provide assistance to those in need who cannot help themselves, such as children or people who are disabled. Those who are capable of helping themselves can receive temporary assistance to meet their basic needs, but they must qualify for benefits. Such hand ups, supporters argue, provide a safety net that keeps people from falling into poverty.

Critics of the welfare system argue that welfare is assistance that is doled out indefinitely to people whose only qualification is being in need. Such handouts, critics

Shriver's job as director of the OEO was to help lift Americans up through the OEO's programs.

say, perpetuate poverty rather than fixing it. Critics point out that despite the money spent on government programs, approximately 15 percent of Americans live in poverty.[2]

IS WELFARE WORTH THE COST?

According to the National Center for Policy Analysis, the United States has spent $22 trillion on antipoverty programs since Johnson declared war on poverty in 1964. That is three times as much as the cost of military wars since the American Revolution (1775–1783). Welfare spending is now $1 trillion each year, including spending by state and local governments.[3]

Critics ask how welfare has benefitted Americans when more than 46 million people still live below the poverty line. Proponents of welfare point out that the safety net has lifted millions of people out of poverty. In 2012, for example,

"WE HAVE BEEN DEFINING SUCCESS AS HOW MUCH MONEY ARE WE SPENDING. . . . WHY DON'T WE THINK ABOUT MEASURING SUCCESS IN THE WAR ON POVERTY BY HOW MANY PEOPLE ARE WE GETTING OUT OF POVERTY? HOW MANY PEOPLE ARE GETTING ON THEIR OWN TWO FEET?"[4]

—HOUSE SPEAKER PAUL RYAN, CONSERVATIVE POLITICAL ACTION CONFERENCE, 2016

THE COST OF WELFARE IN 2015

PROGRAM	FEDERAL SPENDING IN BILLIONS OF DOLLARS[5]
Medicaid	333
EITC and CTC	82
Supplemental Nutritional Assistance Program (SNAP)	79
Supplemental Security Income (SSI)	57
Housing Assistance	48
Pell Grants	32
Temporary Assistance for Needy Families (TANF)	17
Child Nutrition	21
Head Start	10
Job Training	6
Women, Infants, and Children (WIC)	6
Child Care	5
Low Income Home Energy Assistance Program	3

SNAP lifted 10.3 million Americans above the poverty line, and EITC had a similar impact.[6]

Critics of welfare argue that government handouts encourage people not to work because increasing their income might decrease their benefits. Although TANF requirements have addressed the issue of work incentives, proponents of welfare also agree on the need for reform. If welfare programs provide benefits that are higher than the entry-level wages a worker with limited skills can expect to earn, the programs will never succeed in making people self-sufficient. However, research shows the safety net can provide some unexpected results—it allows people to take risks. The availability of welfare, even if it is not used, provides people with the courage to start

REQUIREMENTS FOR OBTAINING WELFARE

Applying for TANF benefits can be a complicated process. Each state has its own requirements, and those seeking benefits must meet both federal and state requirements. In general, applicants must provide information about each family member for whom they are seeking benefits. This includes proof of identity and residence, Social Security benefits received, employment, and other documents, depending on state requirements. Resources, such as a car or savings, may be considered in determining whether an applicant qualifies for aid. After filling out paperwork, applicants are interviewed, and a caseworker determines the benefits for which they qualify. Since employment is required for TANF, applicants are also provided with job assistance if needed. If an application is approved, benefits usually start within 30 to 45 days.

their own businesses. Entrepreneurship can be daunting, but having government programs in place to help them if they fail encourages people to take the risk. And new businesses help the economy grow.

WHAT IS THE GOVERNMENT'S ROLE?

The debate over who should be responsible for providing welfare generally splits along political party lines. Democrats believe the government should be responsible for welfare programs to help people in poverty meet their basic needs. They feel these programs should be supported by tax dollars. Republicans support the need for welfare to help people who live in poverty, but they favor less government spending. They feel private organizations should be responsible for welfare programs.

A HAND IN

The majority of people in poverty are not looking for a handout. They may need a temporary hand up, but what they really want is a hand in. They want to be involved in deciding what to do about it. Empowering the poor to find solutions to their problems dates back to Shriver's leadership in the 1960s. He believed poor people had a right to one-third of the positions on every local community action agency. As stakeholders, these people are qualified to oversee the effectiveness of existing programs and propose improvements to the welfare system.

Members of both parties promote social mobility—the idea that people who are born in poverty should not be stuck in poverty. For Democrats, the answer lies in government investments in education, jobs, and health care. This view is based on the idea that poverty results from barriers, such as lack of jobs that pay adequate wages. For Republicans, government interference promotes welfare dependency instead of self-sufficiency. This view is based on the idea that poverty results from individuals making poor choices, such as choosing to live on welfare instead of working. Differing viewpoints about government spending on welfare is one reason why federal budget proposals are often caught up in Congress.

An instructor, *right*, supervises a student during an antipoverty job training session.

Federally funded programs such as TANF and SNAP are administered through individual states. The debate over the responsibility for welfare spending impacts state governments as well. Republicans favor strict controls on benefits, such as outlawing the use of welfare funds to buy chips, soft drinks, seafood, and steak. Democrats criticize such actions as demeaning to welfare recipients who use their money to feed their families. They point out that only one cent of every SNAP dollar is fraudulently used.

"IF THE PEOPLE CANNOT TRUST THEIR GOVERNMENT TO DO THE JOB FOR WHICH IT EXISTS—TO PROTECT THEM AND TO PROMOTE THEIR COMMON WELFARE—ALL ELSE IS LOST."[7]

—SENATOR BARACK OBAMA, 2006

WHAT IS THE ALTERNATIVE TO GOVERNMENT WELFARE?

Churches and local nonprofit organizations play a large role in providing help to those in need. Republicans propose shrinking the government safety net and allowing private charities to take over the responsibility for welfare. They point out that government programs have not reduced poverty and have not made people self-sufficient. They argue that government programs are often wasteful due to fraud and misuse of funds. Charities, on the other hand, have a better record of using their funds in the way the donations were intended.

Democrats argue that charities cannot replace the safety net. Total donations to charities in 2014 were approximately $360 billion.[8] That is close to what the government spent on 13 welfare programs. If charities could pick up the slack for government cutbacks, Democrats argue, the recession beginning in 2007 would have provided a perfect opportunity. However, charitable donations fell by approximately 13 percent during that time, reducing funds charities could use for welfare programs.[9]

GOVERNMENT VS. CHARITY: ANOTHER VIEW

Most people agree the federal government should be responsible for large welfare programs, such as Social Security, Medicare, and unemployment insurance. These programs are meant for everyone who has contributed to them through taxes. Some argue that charity cannot replace government in providing other, less costly programs for the poor. Others have a different view. Although charities cannot take over responsibility for all welfare, they are uniquely qualified to do a better job of handling some programs. Proponents of this view argue that government cannot replace charity in programs that require working with individuals on specific needs. For example, studies indicate that local nonprofit organizations have a higher success rate than large government programs in providing job training and health clinics.

GLOBAL POVERTY

The concept of global poverty began gaining attention after World War II (1939–1945) when international organizations, such as the World Bank and the United Nations, came into existence. In his 1949 inaugural address, President Harry S. Truman invited other countries to join the United States in helping the less fortunate people of the world achieve a decent, satisfying life.

Nearly 70 years later, countries were still fighting the war on global poverty, but progress had been made. In 2015, World Bank President Jim Yong Kim invited world leaders and financial institutions to join in an effort to end extreme global poverty by 2030.

Refugees in Europe struggle to get by as they wait for shelter and food.

> "MORE THAN HALF THE PEOPLE IN THE WORLD ARE LIVING IN CONDITIONS APPROACHING MISERY. . . . FOR THE FIRST TIME IN HISTORY, HUMANITY POSSESSES THE KNOWLEDGE AND SKILL TO RELIEVE THE SUFFERING OF THOSE PEOPLE."[1]
>
> **—PRESIDENT HARRY TRUMAN, INAUGURAL ADDRESS, 1949**

COMPARING NATIONS

Ranking the nations of the world according to wealth presents many challenges. Depending upon which measurement is used, the results can be very different. Using the wealth of average citizens may provide a more accurate comparison than using the total wealth of a nation.

The same measurement can be used to rank the world's poorest nations, but that does not tell the whole story. Poverty is generally measured by a poverty line. People whose incomes fall below that line are considered poor. However, the cost of meeting basic needs differs from one part of the world to another, so poverty lines vary.

To measure global poverty, a common poverty line must be established, and the unit of measure must be expressed in common terms. In October 2015, the World Bank set the international poverty line at $1.90 per day.

RICH AND POOR NATIONS IN 2015

RICHEST NATIONS	POOREST NATIONS[2]
1. Qatar	1. Democratic Republic of Congo
2. Macao SAR, China	2. Burundi
3. Luxembourg	3. Malawi
4. Kuwait	4. Liberia
5. Singapore	5. Niger
6. Brunei Darussalam	6. Central African Republic
7. Norway	7. Mozambique
8. United Arab Emirates	8. Guinea
9. Switzerland	9. Ethiopia
10. Bermuda	10. Togo

"AMONG RICH COUNTRIES, THE US IS EXCEPTIONAL. WE ARE EXCEPTIONAL IN OUR TOLERANCE OF POVERTY."[5]

—SHELDON DANZIGER, DIRECTOR OF THE NATIONAL POVERTY CENTER AT THE UNIVERSITY OF MICHIGAN

Based on this measure, the World Bank estimated approximately 700 million people in the world lived in extreme poverty.

CHARACTERISTICS OF THE WORLD'S POOR

The highest percentages of people in extreme poverty live in sub-Saharan Africa, the Far East, and Latin America. In 2014, the five countries with the greatest number of poor people were India, China, Nigeria, Bangladesh, and the Democratic Republic of Congo. Some countries with smaller populations had a higher percentage of people living in poverty. For example, Liberia, Burundi, and Madagascar each had an 80 percent poverty rate.[3]

Approximately 70 percent of the world's poorest people lived in rural areas and depended on agriculture to meet their needs.[4] Most lacked access to clean water and did not have adequate sanitation. Many deaths of children were due to hunger-related diseases.

CHILDHOOD POVERTY

To determine rankings for child poverty, the United Nations compared the percentage of children living in a household whose income is less than half of their nation's median income. Based on that measurement, the United States ranked second in the world for the number of children living in poverty in 2012.

Poverty is not only about the money. To measure childhood poverty in European countries, the United Nations Children's Emergency Fund (UNICEF) created a list of 14 items that contribute to the quality of a child's life. The items include basic nutrition—three meals a day that provide protein, fresh fruit, and vegetables. Clothing needs include some new clothes and two pairs of shoes

UNICEF provides necessities for families living in poverty around the world.

suited to the weather. Other items include books, games, toys, regular exercise, and opportunities to celebrate special occasions and invite friends home to play. Childhood poverty levels are measured by the percentage of children in a country who lack two or more items on the list because their families cannot afford to provide them. By this measurement, the percentage of children living in poverty ranged from less than one percent in Iceland to 73 percent in Romania.[6]

REDUCING CHILDHOOD POVERTY IN THE UNITED KINGDOM

In 1999, British Prime Minister Tony Blair made a commitment to end child poverty in the United Kingdom within a generation. Despite changes in leadership since then, UK policymakers continued to expand funding for antipoverty programs aimed at reducing child poverty. Similar to the United States, the United Kingdom had a safety net that includes programs to promote employment and higher wages. However, UK spending on benefits to low-income families exceeded US spending on similar programs by 50 percent.[7] The success of UK efforts to reduce childhood poverty indicates the importance of national commitment and increased spending to strengthen welfare safety nets.

COMPARING SAFETY NETS

Among industrialized nations, poverty rates are tied to the strength of their safety nets—government assistance to the poor. This fact is illustrated by a comparison of childhood poverty rates in the United States and the United Kingdom.

In the late 1990s, both nations had similar child poverty rates of approximately 15 percent. By 2009, the rate in the United Kingdom had fallen to around 12 percent, while the rate in the United States had risen to almost 21 percent.[8] The difference was that the United Kingdom set a national goal of reducing childhood poverty and committed government spending to accomplish it.

An international comparison of developed countries in the late 2000s showed the United States had a higher poverty rate than its peers. Differences in poverty rates, according to the Organisation for Economic Co-operation and Development (OECD), were due solely to government safety nets. The percent of government spending dedicated to safety-net programs was significantly less in the United States than in other rich nations. Some of these countries spend approximately 6 percent of national income on the nonelderly and families with children.

PROGRESS REPORT

In the early 1990s, approximately 2 billion people in the world lived in extreme poverty, based on the World Bank's definition of $1.00 per person per day. By 2012, the number had decreased to 1 billion.[9] By 2015, the number was down to 700 million, and more than 60 developing countries had a decrease in the number of extreme poor.[10] Other positive indicators included an increase in female literacy, a decrease in infant deaths, and widespread improvements in basic health.

GLOBAL PARTNERSHIPS

In 2000, leaders from 189 countries signed the United Nations Millennium Declaration. By adopting this agreement, leaders committed to a global partnership to reduce extreme poverty. They set eight measurable targets with specific deadlines, which became the Millennium Development Goals (MDG). The targets included hunger, education, gender equality, child mortality, health, and the environment. The world made significant progress in achieving the MDGs. For example, the goal of cutting world hunger in half by the end of 2015 was met in many regions of the world. In 2015, world leaders adopted a set of 17 Sustainable Development Goals (SDG), which replace and build on the MDG. The new goals address broader targets, aimed at ending poverty, reducing inequality and injustice, and combating climate change by 2030.

Despite progress, the fight against extreme poverty is far from over. Data was not available for many developing countries, so their progress, or lack of progress, was unknown. Much of the success in poverty reduction was due to China's remarkable decrease in its extreme-poverty rate from more than 80 percent in 1980 to approximately 10 percent in 2015.[11] A large part of China's success was due to moving from collective agriculture to individual farming, which allowed farmers to profit from their work.

Many believe ending extreme global poverty by 2030 is achievable, but success will depend on meeting sustainable development goals through international cooperation. Countries adopted the 17 sustainable development goals in 2015, and each goal had specific targets to be accomplished in the next 15 years. Goals include ending poverty and hunger, promoting good health and quality education, and protecting Earth's ecosystems.

A SUCCESS STORY

Colombia, a country on the northwestern coast of South America, is known for rain forests, towering mountains, and coffee plantations. For the past 50 years, it has been the site of armed conflicts, internal struggles, and widespread poverty. In recent years, Colombia has become known for another reason—its success in the fight against poverty. According to the World Bank, extreme poverty rates were cut in half between 2002 and 2014.[12] Inequalities still exist between urban and rural areas, but many plans are in place to help poor families escape poverty. Lands are being restored to people who had to abandon them because of armed conflict. Women are playing a major role as business owners and managers. Programs are helping children learn violence prevention skills through art, music, and sports.

FROM THE HEADLINES

A STRATEGY TO END POVERTY

In the war on global poverty, 2015 was a very good year. In April, the president of the World Bank outlined a strategy to end extreme poverty: "Grow, Invest, Insure."[13] President Kim said the strategy involved increasing agricultural productivity; providing access to energy, irrigation, and markets; promoting trade; investing in health and education programs for women and children; and providing social safety nets to protect against the impact of natural disasters and epidemics.

Although the strategy was ambitious, Kim said the end of extreme poverty was within reach. The goal would require substantial investments from international banks and the collaboration of governments and citizens. He stated, "The decisions we make this year . . . will help determine whether we have a chance to reach our goal of ending extreme poverty in just 15 years."[14]

In September 2015, leaders from more than 150 nations were joined by heads of corporations and financial institutions at the United Nations Sustainable Development Summit in New York. Attendees included Pope Francis, Nobel Peace Prize winner Malala Yousafzai, UNICEF ambassadors, and many other celebrities and

President Obama spoke to the United Nations Sustainable Development Summit in 2015.

dignitaries. Through the plans adopted at this meeting, world leaders pledged to end extreme global poverty by 2030.

Based on the progress of the previous 25 years, during which extreme global poverty decreased from 37 percent to 10 percent of the world's population, the 2030 goal seemed reachable.[15] The year 2015 reminded the world that all people must work together to solve global problems.

CHAPTER EIGHT

WINNING OR LOSING?

The year 2014 marked the fiftieth anniversary of the War on Poverty and provided an opportunity to evaluate its progress—or lack of progress—in achieving the goals established in 1964. Government programs lifted an average of 27 million people out of poverty each year between 1967 and 2012. Poverty rates fell from 25.8 percent to 16 percent.[1]

When viewed from a different perspective, the War on Poverty was a dismal failure. For the more than $22 trillion the government spent on antipoverty programs in 50 years, progress had been minimal.[2] Attempts to reduce the causes of poverty rather than ease its consequences had failed completely.

According to some statistics, the United States was winning the War on Poverty in 2014.

HONEYCOMB
Honey-comb

Regardless of whether the original goals of the War on Poverty had been met, the battle against poverty continues. In 2016, more than 45 million Americans lived in poverty.[3] The challenge is to determine which antipoverty methods work best and build on their success.

HOW HAS POVERTY CHANGED IN 50 YEARS?

The difficulty of measuring the success or failure of the War on Poverty is that poverty has changed. The age groups, locations, and family structures of those in poverty are different today than in the 1960s.

Poverty rates among people ages 65 and older have dropped substantially since the 1960s, largely due to Social Security programs. Childhood poverty, for people under the age of 18, has experienced ups and downs in the past 50 years, but it has increased since 2000. The number of people living in poverty has decreased slightly in the southern United States, but it has increased in

"THE MOST IMPORTANT LESSON FROM THE WAR ON POVERTY IS THAT GOVERNMENT PROGRAMS AND POLICIES CAN LIFT PEOPLE FROM POVERTY; INDEED THEY HAVE FOR THE PAST 50 YEARS."[4]

—COUNCIL OF ECONOMIC ADVISERS, PROGRESS REPORT ON THE WAR ON POVERTY, 2014

A homeless camp lines a street in Los Angeles, California.

the West. The greatest geographic change has been the significant increase in suburban poverty, which grew more than 50 percent between 2000 and 2010.[5]

Single-parent families are more likely to be poor than two-parent families because there is only one wage earner. Since the 1960s, the number of single-parent families has tripled. The poverty rate for single-mother families in 2014 was almost 40 percent. Approximately 22 percent of families headed by a single dad lived in poverty. Only 8 percent of two-parent families lived below the poverty line.[6]

WINNING

Those who believed the United States was winning the War on Poverty pointed to the successes of federal programs. According to the Council of Economic Advisers' 2014 Progress Report on the War on Poverty, the most successful programs were Social Security, EITC, and SNAP.

Social Security benefits reduced the poverty rate by almost 40 percent among people aged 65 and older. EITC and CTC reduced the childhood poverty rate by approximately 7 percent. And SNAP reduced poverty

A family receives a meal at a Salvation Army center in Detroit, Michigan.

by 2 percent among all recipients and 3 percent among children.[7]

Proponents of the welfare system proclaimed that the federal safety net prevented millions of people from falling into poverty. In addition, they said, programs improved life for those below the poverty line. They pointed to additional people using Medicaid and the Affordable Care Act, increased income for disabled people based on Supplemental Social Security, and greater accessibility to education as a result of Pell Grants.

THE DOE FUND

The Doe Fund is a nonprofit organization that started in New York in 1985. Its original mission was to help homeless people become self-sufficient. George and Harriet McDonald, founders of the Doe Fund, believed, "To solve homelessness for a night, you need shelter. To solve it for good, you need work."[8] Doe Fund programs have provided tens of thousands of homeless people with tools to build a productive life. Through Ready, Willing & Able, individuals earn pay for transitional work while they receive education and job training to enter the workforce. Safe, comfortable shelters and meals are provided, and individuals are offered a variety of affordable housing opportunities. The Doe Fund also offers specialized programs to help veterans, recent parolees, young adults, and low-income families. The organization has a proven track record of giving individuals the hand up they need to become successful members of society.

LOSING

Those who believed the United States was losing the War on Poverty pointed to the more than 45 million Americans who still lived in poverty in

2015. According to US Census Bureau report, 21 percent of Americans participated in a means-tested government welfare program each month in 2012.[9] Participation rates were highest for Medicaid and SNAP.

Based on data between 2009 and 2012, the report indicated the length of time people participated in programs varied. Most people who received benefits from Medicaid, SNAP, or housing assistance participated between three and four years.

Opponents of the welfare system proclaimed that handouts had made people dependent on the government. While spending on means-tested programs had soared, they added, the official poverty rate had remained almost the same since 1967.

"THE VAST MAJORITY OF AMERICANS WHO HAVE EMERGED FROM POVERTY IN THE LAST 50 YEARS HAVE DONE SO BY MEANS OTHER THAN GOVERNMENT PROGRAMS."[10]

—JAY W. RICHARDS, BEST-SELLING AUTHOR AND PROFESSOR OF BUSINESS AND ECONOMICS

IDENTIFYING PROBLEMS AND FINDING SOLUTIONS

Although the War on Poverty helped relieve some symptoms of poverty, Johnson's stated goals went beyond relief.

He said, "Our aim is not only to relieve the symptom of poverty, but to cure it and, above all, to prevent it."[11] Measured against those goals, the war had been lost.

Despite failures, policymakers learned from 50 years of fighting poverty. They debated ways of reforming welfare programs and several recommendations emerged. Some of them sound remarkably similar to the original goals of the War on Poverty: strengthen the economy, provide short-term assistance to those who need it most, and promote self-sufficiency.

Ways of strengthening the economy include bringing good-paying jobs back to the United States and investing in manufacturing. The working poor need jobs that pay a living wage rather than part-time work at minimum wages and no benefits.

Able-bodied adults should be required to work or train for work in order to receive benefits from welfare programs. This requirement instills a sense of pride in work and provides an incentive to become self-sufficient.

Investing in education, especially early childhood education, is an important weapon to break the cycle of poverty. Research indicated successful results for children

EDUCATION AND WELFARE

Lyndon Johnson called education "our primary weapon in the war on poverty and the principal tool for building a Great Society."[12] His 1965 legislation included Head Start, which was designed to give preschool children educational, social, and cultural experiences. Upward Bound provided support for low-income high school students in preparation for college entrance. Adult Basic Education provided illiterate or uneducated adults with instruction in reading, writing, and math to qualify them for jobs. The fact that all these programs still exist supports Johnson's belief that "Poverty must not be a bar to learning, and learning must offer an escape from poverty."[13] Congress reauthorized the Elementary and Secondary Education Act of 1965 several times, most recently in 2015 when President Obama signed the Every Student Succeeds Act. This law governs US education policy and requires schools to prepare students for college and careers. Obama said, "With this bill, we reaffirm that fundamentally American ideal—that every child . . . deserves the chance to make of their lives what they will."[14]

who participated in the Head Start program, which was part of the original War on Poverty. They were more likely to finish high school, attend college, and avoid many of the problems associated with being raised in poverty.

CAN POVERTY BE PREVENTED?

Poverty can be relieved. Without question, the safety net works. Current data show government programs reduced poverty in the United States from 26 percent in 1967 to 15 percent in 2014. The safety net prevented 41 million Americans who would otherwise have been poor from slipping below the poverty line in 2014.[15] Many of the programs that continue to address problems today have their roots in Johnson's War on Poverty.

In the war on global poverty, remarkable achievements were also made. In 1990, approximately 37 percent of the world's population lived in extreme poverty. In 2015, according to the World Bank, the number was less than 10 percent.[16] The pledge of world leaders to end extreme global poverty by 2030 provided hope for reaching the goal etched on the World Bank headquarters: "Our Dream is a World Free of Poverty."

A PROGRAM THAT WORKS

The Maternal, Infant, and Early Childhood Home Visiting (MIECHV) program was created in 2010, and funding was extended through 2017. Through MIECHV, each state supports local agencies that provide home visits by health, social service, and child development professionals to low-income families in their homes. These professionals address problems such as health, safety, and nutrition. They teach young mothers skills they lack, such as how to care for babies. They improve relationships within a family and provide strategies for better parenting of older children. Although the program has not been in existence for long, preliminary evidence shows promising results. MIECHV reduced developmental problems and mental health issues for children and decreased calls to child welfare authorities. Families reported less stress at home, which gave parents the ability to focus on helping their children succeed.

ESSENTIAL FACTS

MAJOR EVENTS

- In January 1964, the United States begins waging a War on Poverty, not only to relieve the symptoms of poverty but also to cure and prevent it.
- In August 1996, the Personal Responsibility and Work Opportunity Act changes government welfare into a system that requires work in exchange for time-limited benefits.
- In November 2012, New York City fast-food workers begin the "Fight for $15," which becomes a nationwide movement to raise the minimum wage.
- In 2015, world leaders pledge to end extreme global poverty by 2030.

KEY PLAYERS

- Lyndon B. Johnson launches the Great Society—a set of programs aimed at improving the environment, increasing educational opportunities, and eliminating poverty in the United States.

- Sargent Shriver becomes head of the Office of Economic Opportunity and director of the War on Poverty, responsible for carrying out the largest expansion of government assistance programs in history.
- Barack Obama signs the Affordable Care Act, sweeping changes in health-care benefits for low-income people that expanded access to health insurance for those who were previously uninsured due to the high cost of coverage.

IMPACT ON SOCIETY

The original goals of the War on Poverty were to lift people out of poverty and enable them to become self-sufficient. Although 50 years of government antipoverty programs succeeded in relieving the symptoms of poverty, they failed to address its causes. In 2016, more than 45 million Americans lived in poverty, and the United States ranked second out of thirty-five in the world in childhood poverty. Government leaders pledged to reform federal safety net programs.

QUOTE

"The simplest description of the War on Poverty is that it is a means of making life available for any and all pursuers. . . . The War on Poverty tries only to create the conditions by which the good life can be lived."

—Sargent Shriver, 1964

GLOSSARY

DEMOCRAT

A member of the Democratic political party. Democrats believe in social change and strong government.

MEANS-TESTED PROGRAM

A welfare program that is free to anyone who qualifies for the benefits, usually based on income level.

MEDICAID

A US program that provides access to health-care benefits for low-income families and individuals.

MEDICARE

A US program that provides health-care coverage for people ages 65 and older.

MINIMUM WAGE

The lowest wage permitted by law.

POVERTY LINE

A minimum income below which an individual or family is classified as living in poverty.

PRECINCT

A voting district of a city or town.

RECESSION

A period of negative economic growth and, usually, low demand for goods and high unemployment.

REPUBLICAN

A member of the Republican political party. Republicans are conservative and believe in small government.

SOCIAL SECURITY

A US program started in the 1930s to provide retirement income for people over the age of 65.

STANDARD OF LIVING

A level of wealth and quality of life.

SUPPLEMENTAL POVERTY MEASURE

An alternative way of determining poverty levels that includes the value of noncash assistance provided by the government, as well as a household's taxes, work-related expenses, and out-of-pocket medical expenses.

ADDITIONAL RESOURCES

SELECTED BIBLIOGRAPHY

Matthews, Dylan. "Everything You Need to Know About the War on Poverty." *Washington Post*. Washington Post, 8 Jan. 2014. Web. 23 May 2016.

Radelet, Steven. "Progress in the Global War on Poverty." *Christian Science Monitor*. Christian Science Monitor, 7 Feb. 2016. Web. 23 May 2016.

Williams, Joseph P. "Going from Middle Class to Poverty." *US News*. US News & World Report, 6 Jan. 2014. Web. 23 May 2016.

FURTHER READINGS

Duncan, Cynthia M. *Worlds Apart: Poverty and Politics and Rural America*. New Haven, CT: Yale UP, 2014. Print.

Edin, Kathryn J., and H. Luke Shaefer. *$2.00 a Day: Living on Almost Nothing in America*. Boston: Houghton, 2015. Print.

WEBSITES

To learn more about Special Reports, visit **booklinks.abdopublishing.com**. These links are routinely monitored and updated to provide the most current information available.

FOR MORE INFORMATION

For more information on this subject, contact or visit the following organizations:

AmeriCorps VISTA
250 E Street, SW
Washington, DC 20525
800-833-3722
http://www.nationalservice.gov/programs/americorps/americorps-vista
AmeriCorps VISTA provides opportunities for volunteers who make a commitment to assist low-income communities through working on projects that help bring individuals out of poverty.

Feeding America
35 East Wacker Drive, Suite 2000
Chicago, IL 60601
800-771-2303
http://www.feedingamerica.org
Feeding America is a nonprofit organization that provides food for people in need through a nationwide system of food banks.

SOURCE NOTES

CHAPTER 1. WHO ARE THE POOR?

1. Alvin Major. "Winning $15 an Hour Means Everything to Me." *CNBC*. CNBC, 23 July 2015. Web. 23 May 2016.

2. Joseph Pisani. "Fast-Food Workers Protest Nationwide for $15 Minimum Wage." *Portland Press Herald*. MaineToday Media, 10 Nov. 2015. Web. 23 May 2016.

3. Paul Davidson. "Fast-Food Workers Strike, Seeking $15 Wage, Political Muscle." *USA Today*. USA Today, 10 Nov. 2015. Web. 23 May 2016.

4. Chris Kirkham and Samantha Masunaga. "Why the Success of the $15 Minimum Wage Movement Has Surprised Its Leaders." *Los Angeles Times*. Los Angeles Times, 11 Nov. 2015. Web. 23 May 2016.

5. Michael Harrington. *The Other America; Poverty in the United States*. New York: Macmillan, 1962. 528.

6. Maurice Isserman. "Michael Harrington: Warrior on Poverty." *New York Times*. New York Times, 19 June 2009. Web. 23 May 2016.

7. "Annual Update of the HHS Poverty Guidelines." *Federal Register*. Federal Register, 25 Jan. 2016. Web. 23 May 2016.

8. Elise Gould, Tanyell Cooke, and Will Kimball. "What Families Need to Get By: EPI's 2015 Family Budget Calculator." *Economic Policy Institute*. Economic Policy Institute, 26 Aug. 2015. Web. 23 May 2016.

9. Katey Troutman. "How Much Money Does the Middle Class Really Need to Get By?" *Money & Career CheatSheet*. CheatSheet, 9 Dec. 2015. Web. 23 May 2016.

10. Elise Gould, Tanyell Cooke, and Will Kimball. "What Families Need to Get By: EPI's 2015 Family Budget Calculator." *Economic Policy Institute*. Economic Policy Institute, 26 Aug. 2015. Web. 23 May 2016.

CHAPTER 2. CAUSES OF POVERTY

1. "US Poverty Statistics." *Federal Safety Net*. Federal Safety Net, n.d. Web. 23 May 2016.

2. "Increases in Homelessness on the Horizon." *National Alliance to End Homelessness*. National Alliance to End Homelessness, 28 Sept. 2011. Web. 23 May 2016.

3. Eric M Johnson. "More than 500,000 People Homeless in the United States: Report." *Reuters*. Reuters, 19 Nov. 2015. Web. 23 May 2016.

4. "Child Poverty." *National Center for Children in Poverty*. Columbia University, 2016. Web. 23 May 2016.

5. Emily Cuddy, Joanna Venator, and Richard V. Reeves. "In a Land of Dollars: Deep Poverty and Its Consequences." *Brookings*. The Brookings Institution, 7 May 2015. Web. 23 May 2016.

6. Ibid.

7. "US Poverty Statistics." *Federal Safety Net*. Federal Safety Net, n.d. Web. 23 May 2016.

8. "Economic Security for Seniors Facts." *NCOA*. NCOA, n.d. Web. 23 May 2016.

9. Roseanne L. Flores. "A War on Children: The Consequences of Poverty on Child Development." *American Psychological Association*. APA, 21 Oct. 2014. Web. 23 May 2016.

10. Victoria A. Brownworth. "The Invisible Americans." *HuffPost Politics*. Huffington Post, 7 Apr. 2014. Web. 23 May 2016.

11. "US Poverty Statistics." *Federal Safety Net*. Federal Safety Net, n.d. Web. 23 May 2016.

CHAPTER 3. DECLARING WAR ON POVERTY

1. "State of the Union Address, 1964." *PBS*. WGBH Educational, 8 Jan. 1964. Web. 23 May 2016.

2. Ibid.

3. "History of Community Action." *IACAA*. Illinois Association of Community Action Agencies, 2016. Web. 23 May 2016.

4. "The Legacy of the War on Poverty." *Shriver Center*. Shriver Center, n.d. Web. 23 May 2016.

5. Ibid.

6. Scott Stossel. "The Good Works of Sargent Shriver." *Atlantic*. Atlantic Monthly Group, 18 Jan. 2011. Web. 23 May 2016.

7. Bob Powell. "March 9, 1965: President Lyndon Johnson Signs Bill to Create Appalachian Regional Commission." *West Virginia Public Broadcasting*. West Virginia Public Broadcasting, 9 Mar. 2015. Web. 23 May 2016.

8. Joseph A. Califano Jr. "What Was Really Great about the Great Society." *Washington Monthly*. Washington Monthly, Oct. 1999. Web 23 May 2016.

CHAPTER 4. PROGRAMS FOR THE POOR

1. "TANF." *Federal Safety Net*. Federal Safety Net, n.d. Web. 23 May 2016.

2. Sasha Abramsky. *The American Way of Poverty: How the Other Half Still Lives*. New York: Nation, 2013. Print. 55.

3. "Annual Report 2014–2015." *DuPagePads*. DuPagePads, n.d. Web. 23 May 2016.

CHAPTER 5. POLITICS AND POVERTY

1. Ronald Reagan. "Address before a Joint Session of Congress on the State of the Union." *American Presidency Project*. Gerhard Peters and John T. Woolley, 2016. Web. 23 May 2016.

2. Arthur C. Brooks. *The Conservative Heart: How to Build a Fairer, Happier, and More Prosperous America*. New York: Broadside, 2015. Print. 70.

3. Leigh Ann Caldwell. "Republican Candidates Turn to the Issue of Poverty. But Does Anyone Care?" *NBC News*. NBCNews.com, 8 Jan. 2016. Web. 23 May 2016.

4. Jordan Malter. "Why Poor People Still Aren't Voting." *CNN*. Cable News Network, 5 Aug. 2015. Web. 23 May 2016.

5. "Remarks on Signing the Tax Reform Act (October 22, 1986)." *Miller Center*. Rector and Visitors of the University of Virginia, 2016. Web. 23 May 2016.

6. Daniel Weeks. "Why Are the Poor and Minorities Less Likely to Vote?" *Atlantic*. Atlantic Monthly Group, 10 Jan. 2014. Web. 23 May 2016.

7. Stephen Lurie. "Why It Matters That Politicians Have No Experience of Poverty." *Atlantic*. Atlantic Monthly Group, 2 June 2014. Web. 23 May 2016.

8. "Snapshot of Homelessness." *National Alliance to End Homelessness*. National Alliance to End Homelessness, 2016. Web. 23 May 2016.

9. Tianna Gaines-Turner. "Three Steps We Can Take to Solve Poverty from Someone Who Knows Firsthand." *Moyers & Company*. Public Square Media, 11 July 2014. Web. 23 May 2016.

SOURCE NOTES CONTINUED

10. Greg Kaufmann. "This Week in Poverty: The Expert Testimony of Tianna Gaines-Turner." *Nation*. Nation, 9 Aug. 2013. Web. 23 May 2016.

CHAPTER 6. HAND UP OR HANDOUT?

1. "Papers of Lyndon B. Johnson." *American Presidency Project*. Gerhard Peters and John T. Woolley, 2016. Web. 23 May 2016.

2. Louis Woodhill. "The War on Poverty Wasn't a Failure—It Was a Catastrophe." *Forbes*. Forbes, 19 Mar. 2014. Web. 23 May 2016.

3. Mike Konczal. "No, We Don't Spend $1 Trillion on Welfare Each Year." *Washington Post*. Washington Post, 12 Jan. 2014. Web. 23 May 2016.

4. David Sherfinski. "Paul Ryan at CPAC: Solutions for Combating Poverty Lie with Local Communities." *Washington Times*. Washington Times, 3 Mar. 2016. Web. 23 May 2016.

5. "Social Safety Net." *Federal Safety Net*. Federal Safety Net, n.d. Web. 23 May 2016.

6. Arloc Sherman and Danilo Trisi. "Safety Net More Effective against Poverty Than Previously Thought." *Center on Budget and Policy Priorities*. Center on Budget and Policy Priorities, 6 May 2016. Web. 23 May 2016.

7. Barack Obama. "Barack Obama's Address to the University of Nairobi: An Honest Government, A Hopeful Future." Embassy of the United States, Nairobi, Kenya. US Department of State, 28 Aug. 2006. Web. 17 Aug. 2016.

8. "Giving Statistics." *Charity Navigator*. Charity Navigator, 2016. Web. 23 May 2016.

9. Mike Konczal. "The Conservative Myth of a Social Safety Net Built on Charity." *Atlantic*. Atlantic Monthly Group, 24 Mar. 2014. Web. 23 May 2016.

CHAPTER 7. GLOBAL POVERTY

1. Harry Truman. "Truman's Inaugural Address." *Harry S. Truman Library and Museum*. Harry S. Truman Library & Museum, n.d. Web. 23 May 2016.

2. "GDP Per Capita, PPP." *World Bank*. World Bank Group, 2016. Web. 23 May 2016.

3. "Ending Poverty Requires More Than Growth, Says WBG." *World Bank*. World Bank Group, 10 Apr. 2015. Web. 23 May 2016.

4. "Know Your World: Facts about Hunger and Poverty." *Hunger Project*. Hunger Project, n.d. Web. 23 May 2016.

5. Saki Knafo. "US Child Poverty Second Highest among Developed Nations: Report." *HuffPost Impact*. Huffington Post, 31 May 2012. Web. 23 May 2016.

6. UNICEF Innocenti Research Centre. "Measuring Child Poverty: New League Tables of Child Poverty in the World's Rich Countries." *UNICEF Innocenti Research Centre.* UNICEF, May 2012. Web. 23 May 2016.

7. Timothy M. Smeeding and Jane Waldfogel. "Fighting Child Poverty in the United States and United Kingdom: An Update." *Fast Focus.* Institute for Research on Poverty, University of Wisconsin–Madison, Dec. 2010. Web. 23 May 2016.

8. Ibid.

9. "World Bank President Outlines Strategy to End Poverty, Welcomes New Development Partners." *World Bank.* World Bank Group, 7 Apr. 2015. Web. 23 May 2016.

10. Steven Radelet. "Progress in the Global War on Poverty." *Christian Science Monitor.* Christian Science Monitor, 7 Feb. 2016. Web. 23 May 2016.

11. Ibid.

12. "Colombia: Winning the War on Poverty and Inequality despite the Odds." *World Bank.* World Bank Group, 14 Jan. 2016. Web. 23 May 2016.

13. "World Bank President Outlines Strategy to End Poverty, Welcomes New Development Partners." *World Bank.* World Bank Group, 7 Apr. 2015. Web. 23 May 2016.

14. Ibid.

15. Alex Thier. "An Astonishing Year for the War on Global Poverty." *Foreign Policy.* Foreign Policy, 8 Jan. 2016. Web. 23 May 2016.

CHAPTER 8. WINNING OR LOSING?

1. "The War on Poverty 50 Years Later: A Progress Report." *Council of Economic Advisors.* White House, Jan. 2014. Web. 23 May 2016.

2. Robert Rector and Rachel Sheffield. "The War on Poverty after 50 Years." *Heritage Foundation.* Heritage Foundation, 15 Sept. 2014. Web. 23 May 2016.

3. Adam Johnson. "45 Million Americans Live in Poverty, but You Wouldn't Know It from Watching 2016 Coverage." *Alternet.* Alternet, 5 Jan. 2016. Web. 23 May 2016.

4. "The War on Poverty 50 Years Later: A Progress Report." *Council of Economic Advisors.* White House, Jan. 2014. Web. 23 May 2016.

5. Peter B. Edelman. *So Rich, So Poor: Why It's So Hard to End Poverty in America.* New York: New Press, 2012. Print. 29.

6. "Historical Poverty Tables—People." *US Census Bureau.* US Department of Commerce, n.d. Web. 23 May 2016.

7. "The War on Poverty 50 Years Later: A Progress Report." *Council of Economic Advisors.* White House, Jan. 2014. Web. 23 May 2016.

8. "Ready Willing & Able." *Doe Fund.* Doe Fund, n.d. Web. 23 May 2016.

9. "21.3 Percent of US Population Participates in Government Assistance Programs Each Month." *US Census Bureau.* US Department of Commerce, 28 May 2015. Web. 23 May 2016.

10. "The War on Poverty at 50." *National Review.* National Review, 8 Jan. 2014. Web. 23 May 2016.

11. "State of the Union Address, 1964." *PBS.* WGBH Educational, 8 Jan. 1964. Web. 23 May 2016.

12. "Weapons Against Poverty: Three Prong Attack." *LBJ for Kids.* LBJ Presidential Library, n.d. Web. 23 May 2016.

13. Ibid.

14. "Every Student Succeeds Act (ESSA)." *US Department of Education.* White House, n.d. Web. 8 April 2016.

15. Sharon Parrott. "Commentary: War on Poverty: Large Positive Impact, but More Work Remains." *Center on Budget and Policy Priorities.* Center on Budget and Policy Priorities, 7 Jan. 2014. Web. 23 May 2016.

16. Alex Thier. "An Astonishing Year for the War on Global Poverty." *Foreign Policy.* Foreign Policy, 8 Jan. 2016. Web. 23 May 2016.

INDEX

ABOUT THE **AUTHOR**

Carolee Laine is an educator and children's writer. She has written social studies textbooks and other educational materials, as well as passages for statewide assessments. She enjoys learning through researching and writing nonfiction books for young readers. Laine lives in the Chicago, Illinois, suburbs.